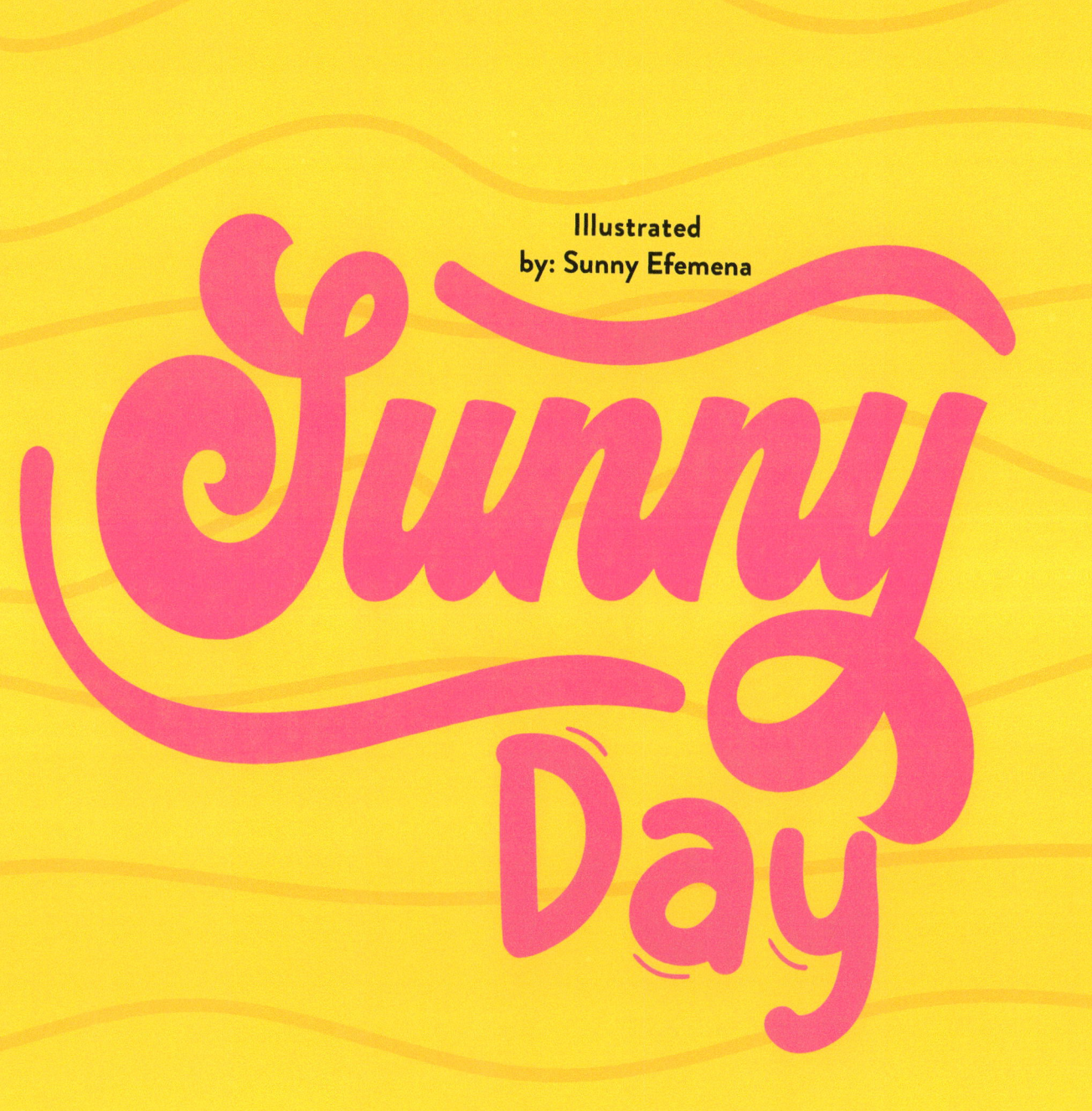

Illustrated by: Sunny Efemena

# Sunny Day

ELEVIV PUBLISHING GROUP

I love sunny days!

Sunny days
Sunny days
I love sunny days.

Sunny days
Sunny days
How I love
sunny days.

How we get to jump on the Trampoline… That's what I love about **sunny days.**

Sunny days
Sunny days
How I love
sunny days.

Sunny days
Sunny days
How I love sunny days.

I love how we can run in the grass
With the wind on my face
That's what I love about
**sunny days.**

Sunny days
Sunny days
How I love
sunny days.

Sunny days
Sunny days
I love sunny days.

# The End

**Sunny Days**
Copyright @ 2021 by Toni Fasidi

All rights reserved. No part of this book may be reproduced or transmitted in any form or by any means without the written permission of the author.

**Illustrated by:**
Sunny Efemena

**Published by:**
Eleviv Publishing Group
www.elevivpublishing.com
info@elevivpublishing.com
1-800-353-0635
1-281-857-0569

**ISBN:** 978-1-952744-18-1
978-1-952744-22-8
978-1-952744-16-7

**Printed in the United States of America**

10 9 8 7 6 5 4 3 2

www.ingramcontent.com/pod-product-compliance
Lightning Source LLC
Chambersburg PA
CBHW050753110526
44592CB00002B/50